MIND & BODY

Written by David Webb

FIRST PUBLISHED IN DECEMBER 2001

by

Educational Printing Services Limited

Albion Mill, Water Street, Great Harwood, Blackburn, BB6 7QR
Telephone: (01254) 882080   Fax: (01254) 882010
e-mail: enquiries@eprint.co.uk   Website: www.eprint.co.uk

ISBN 1 900818 97 3

Introduction

PSHE and Citizenship is different from all other curriculum subjects in that it embraces the development of the whole child - both **Mind and Body**.

The Key Stage 2 non-statutory guidelines for PSHE and Citizenship identify four key areas to be developed in terms of knowledge, skills and understanding. They are:

- Developing confidence and responsibility and making the most of their abilities

- Preparing to play an active role as citizens

- Developing a healthy, safer lifestyle

- Developing good relationships and respecting differences between people.

Mind and Body covers a broad range of key areas selected from the non-statutory guidelines. It encourages children to discuss their own experiences, share their thoughts and express their ideas. It presents thought provoking scenarios and provides opportunities for both writing activities and drama.

Mind and Body is a resource to help children move forward at this key stage in their lives and to encourage them to be mature and responsible citizens who will play a full and active roll in a fair and caring society.

Contents

Contents

Healthy Eating

Healthy eating is essential if you are to lead a full and active life. It is important to achieve a balanced diet as different foods provide different benefits to your body. Food is your fuel and if you do not provide your body with the right mixture it will not operate to its full potential. A regular, well balanced, healthy diet will give you all the energy you need, help fight disease and also help you to look your best

REMEMBER: YOU ARE WHAT YOU EAT.

The Right Balance

Are you confident that you eat a balanced diet?

- Write down everything you ate and drank yesterday, from the time you got up to the time you went to bed. (Use Worksheet 1). Your teacher should do the same exercise on the board/flipchart.

- Your teacher should choose a few children to read out their results. He/she should deliberately choose one child who stays for school dinner and one child who brings a packed lunch.

- To grow up healthy it is important to achieve a good, balanced diet by eating a variety of different foods. Food can be divided into five main groups as follows:

33%
Breads, cereals potatoes

12%
Meat, fish & alternatives

33%
Fruit & Vegetables

15%
Milk & dairy foods

7%
Sugary & fatty foods

- If you eat a good variety of food in the correct proportions from the five groups, your bodies will receive the range of nutrients needed to keep healthy and operate efficiently.

- Look at your list of food and drink and sort each item into one of the five food categories. (Worksheet 1). Discuss the results. Who had a healthy eating day? Who could have done better? How did your teacher do?

Worksheet 1

Make a list of everything you had to eat and drink yesterday, from the moment you got up to the moment you went to bed.

Food diary for a day				
Breakfast	Dinner	Tea	Supper	Snacks

Sort each item on your list into one of the five food categories below.

The right balance?				
Breads, cereals potatoes	Fruit and vegetables	Milk and dairy foods	Meat, fish and alternatives	Sugary and fatty foods

Look at your chart. Do you think you had a good, healthy eating day yesterday?

The Five Main Food Groups

● **Bread, Other Cereals and Potatoes**

> *All types of bread • rice • oats • noodles • pasta*
> *potatoes • beans • peas • lentils*

The food in this group is very good for you. The items are high in fibre and provide good sources of starchy carbohydrate. Most people do not eat enough from this group. You should try to eat at least 4 slices of bread each day (preferably wholemeal or wholegrain) and 2 portions of potatoes, pasta or rice.

● **Fruit and Vegetables**

> *All types of fresh fruit and vegetables • pure fruit juice*
> *frozen, canned and dried fruit and vegetables*

Fruit and vegetables are packed with vitamins and minerals. They are also a good source of fibre as well as being low in fat. Again, most people do not eat enough from this group. You should eat at least five portions of fruit and vegetables every day.

● **Milk and Dairy Foods**

> *Milk • all types of cheese • yoghurt • fromage frais*

The items in this group provide protein and calcium to build strong bones and teeth. However, they can be high in fat - especially saturated fat. You should eat moderate amounts from this group and choose low fat products where possible e.g. skimmed or semi-skimmed milk.

● **Meat, Fish and Alternatives**

> *All fresh meat, poultry and fish*
> *frozen and canned fish • shellfish • soya products*

The food in this group provides a major source of protein, vitamins and minerals. Again, you should eat moderate amounts and try to choose products that are low in fat. Bacon, sausages and beefburgers are not good choices as they have a high fat content and therefore should not be eaten too often. You should try to eat two portions of fish each week. Oily fish, such as tuna, salmon, mackerel or sardines, is better for you.

● Fatty and Sugary Foods

> *Butter, margarine and low fat spreads • cream • ice cream cooking oil • mayonnaise • chocolate • cakes • biscuits sweets • soft drinks • crisps • honey, jam and marmalade*

Most people eat far too much from this group, which is high in sugar content and saturated fat. Eating too much sugar adds calories to your diet and also increases the chances of tooth decay. Taking in too much saturated fat raises the level of cholesterol, which can lead to heart disease. It can also contribute to being overweight.

What does it mean?

Calcium - calcium salts are an essential component of bones and teeth. Foods rich in calcium build strong bones and teeth.

Calories - are used to measure the energy value of food. One slice of white toast would contain about 38 calories, a raw apple would have 81 calories and 1lb of steak would have 785 calories.

Carbohydrates - carbohydrates are made up of starch and sugar. They give us energy. If we eat more than our body needs it will turn to fat.

Cholesterol - occurs naturally in most body tissue, including the blood. Eating too much fatty food can increase cholesterol, which may lead to health problems.

Minerals - most minerals come from the soil. The body needs minerals to build healthy tissue.

Vitamins - are organic compounds essential for normal growth and nutrition. A lack of a particular vitamin (vitamin deficiency) can lead to disease.

Saturated fats - are naturally oily or greasy substances that are present in the body. In food, they occur primarily in animal products such as meat, whole milk, cream and cooking oil. Saturated fats are used by the body to make cholesterol.

Activity Page

Create a Menu

Look at the menu below. This is clearly not a healthy eating menu. Use the blank menu card to create meals for the day that are much more healthy. You should try to achieve a well balanced diet.

MENU CARD

Breakfast	Snack	Lunch	Evening Meal	Supper
Sausage, Egg & Bacon Toast & Plum Jam 2 Cups of Coffee	Jam Doughnut Coffee	Cornish Pastie Chocolate Muffin Coffee	2 Pork Chops, Chips Peas & Gravy Syrup Sponge and Custard	Toasted Crumpets Hot Chocolate made with milk

MENU CARD

Breakfast	Snack	Lunch	Evening Meal	Supper

Which is your favourite?

Not everybody likes the same food. Use the table below to list your favourite foods. Compare your list with your friends.

My Favourites

Breakfast cereal	Fruit	Vegetable	Type of potato	Meat or fish	Pudding	Drink

Now: Collect the data from the rest of the class *(you could use a tally chart for this)* and draw a block graph to show your class's favourite foods.

Exercise

Just as the majority of people do not eat enough healthy food, so the majority of people do not take enough exercise. Exercise is one of the most important things you can do to promote both a healthy mind and a healthy body. Exercise can change how you feel and how you look - and you do not have to be good at sport to exercise. Regular exercise helps you look and feel better and can also reduce the risk of some diseases. It will improve your strength, stamina, skill and suppleness, so improving the quality of your life.

Exercise and How You Feel

Have you noticed that when you are feeling tired or lethargic, taking a walk in the fresh air can liven you up? It makes you feel more alert and also helps you to sleep more soundly. The same is true of playtime at school. You may feel tired, having worked hard at your lessons. A break in the fresh air, when you can run around and play, makes you feel refreshed and ready to get back to work - hopefully! On the other hand, exercise can make you feel more relaxed. If you have been worried or anxious about something, exercise can act as a calming influence, reducing stress and helping you to cope.

Exercise and How You Look

Have you noticed how fit the top sports personalities look? This is no accident. As well as making you feel better, exercise can change the way you look. Regular exercise will strengthen your muscles and increase the flexibility of your joints, thus making you stronger and more supple. An added bonus is that exercise helps blood circulation and so improves the function of your heart and lungs. Exercise burns calories and therefore consumes excess body fat. This keeps your body weight under control.

Activity Page

1. How many different types of exercise can you identify?

Hold a brainstorming session, either as a class, in groups or in pairs, and list as many different types of exercise as possible.

The Four S's

strength • stamina • skill • suppleness

See if you can sort the results of your brainstorming session into the above four categories. (Worksheet 2) You will have to list many forms of exercise under more than one heading, (e.g. football promotes both skill and stamina).

2. What immediate effect does exercise have on your body?

It is best to do this research either in the school hall or outside. You will need a pencil and paper and you will need to have an exercise routine worked out, (e.g. skipping, running, jumping, etc.). You can use Worksheet 2 to record the answers to the questions below.

- Your pulse is a steady throb caused by blood being pumped through your arteries. Practise finding your pulse either on your wrist or on your neck.

- Time your pulse rate for one minute and make a note of it.

- Perform your exercise routine for two or three minutes.

- Sit down and time your pulse rate again. What do you notice?

- Sit still and breathe steadily for two minutes.

- Time your pulse rate again. What do you notice?

- Does the vigorous exercise have any other effects on your body?

> **Tip:** It is important to begin your routine with some warm up exercises. You should gradually increase the intensity of your exercise. You should always allow time for rest and recovery after exercise. It is a good idea to take in some fluid.

Worksheet 2 - Exercise

Different types of exercise			
Strength	Stamina	Skill	Suppleness

What effect does exercise have on your body?

Pulse rate after one minute   =

Pulse rate after exercise   =

Pulse rate after recovery   =

What other effects did the exercise routine have on your body?

Personal Hygiene

A young baby is unable to control its personal hygiene. A baby relies on its mother to change a nappy and to wash and bath it regularly. Gradually, the baby becomes a toddler. The young child becomes toilet trained and learns how to wash and care for him/herself. As the child grows, so personal hygiene becomes more and more important. It is essential to learn good personal hygiene habits and to establish a regular hygiene routine.

Do you know your skin?

Your skin acts as a flexible covering for your body. The surface of your skin is full of little holes called **pores**. When you are hot or when you exercise, your pores open and sweat comes out. In this way, your body cools itself. An oily substance also comes out of your pores and this keeps your skin smooth. There are small hairs on the surface of your skin, which help to protect it and also help to keep you warm. In cold weather, the tiny hairs trap air, which is warmed up by your body.

ACTIVITY

*   Use a magnifying glass to look closely at the skin on your arm.

    Can you see your pores?

    Can you see your small hairs?

    What else can you see? (e.g. moles, scratches).

*   Use the magnifying glass to look at your hands and your fingernails.

    Note down everything you see.

    How clean are your hands and nails?

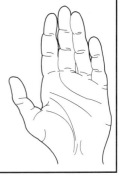

Unhygienic Henry

Henry sat up in bed with a start. His mum had called him more than fifteen minutes ago but he had dozed off to sleep again. He was going to be late for school. Mrs Douglas would go mad. It would be his third time late in a week. He threw aside the bedclothes and rummaged on the floor for his socks and underpants. They were the same socks and underpants he had worn all week - but they would have to do - he was late.

'I'll change them tomorrow,' he said to himself. 'Nobody's going to see them, are they?'

Henry shook the toast crumbs from last night's supper from his underpants and pulled them on. His legs were still grubby from playing football the previous evening. It had been too cold to have a shower.

Henry rushed to the bathroom only to find his sister had beaten him to it. She would take ages. He decided not to bother with a wash - especially as he'd had one last weekend.

Henry's mum had already set off for work but she had left him some cereal and toast on the table. He sat down and gave a huge sneeze - right over his cereal bowl!

'Must be getting a cold,' he muttered, and he wiped his nose on the back of his sleeve.

Henry guzzled his breakfast, spilling some of the milk from his cereal on his already stained trousers, and then he looked around for his school shoes. He thought about brushing his teeth but decided against it. He had toothache and when he had last brushed them, a few days ago, it had really hurt. They were a bit yellow but he was sure nobody would notice.

Henry found his shoes by the front door. They were covered in mud and soaking wet. Never mind, they would dry during the day. He couldn't help but notice a funny, musty smell when he pulled them on but he was sure that would disappear once he got out in the fresh air.

Henry opened the front door and set off for school, wondering why none of his classmates called for him anymore.

Points For Discussion

It is not surprising that nobody wants to walk to school with Henry. He is a hygienic disaster! Use bullet points to make a list of all the hygienic problems you can find in the story.

Why do you think it is important to change your clothes regularly?

Why is it important to shower and wash regularly?

What are the implications if you fail to brush your teeth regularly?

We may be able to laugh at the antics of unhygienic Henry but, in reality, he would be a most unpleasant boy. It is very important to be aware of personal hygiene, particularly as you grow and mature. You should develop regular routines and take responsibility for your own personal hygiene.

DO NOT BECOME AN UNHYGIENIC HENRY OR HENRIETTA!

BE NICE TO KNOW - NOT A MUST TO AVOID!

Living by the Rules

As you live your life, there are certain rules that you are expected to follow. Your parents, or whoever you live with, will expect you to behave in a certain way, or do particular jobs around the house. Similarly, when you are at school, high standards of behaviour and a positive approach to work are expected.

Rules are important. They help your life to run smoothly and efficiently. Can you imagine what life would be like if there were no rules at all?

At Home

• Make a list of rules that you are expected to follow at home. Your list should include rules about behaviour and also jobs that you are expected to do.

• Which two rules do you think are the most important? Put a star by the side of your choices.

• What happens when you break the rules? How do you feel?

At School

• Write down six rules that apply at school.

• Choose any two of the rules you have identified and explain why you think they are necessary.

• Are there any school rules that you think are unnecessary? Give a reason.

Points For Discussion

Some rules are introduced for reasons of safety, some are to establish order and some are just to make life more pleasant. Discuss the different types of rules you have identified.

Talk about the consequences of breaking the rules. What happens when you break the rules at home? What happens when you break the rules at school? Is it necessary to have different punishments for different rules?

What do you think should happen if someone persistently breaks the rules at school?

Are there any additional rules you would like to see introduced at school?

Classroom Code

What sort of a place do you want your classroom to be? How do you want your fellow pupils to behave? Write a paragraph outlining your thoughts and ideas.

Write down six rules that you would like to see implemented in your classroom.

1.

2.

3.

4.

5.

6.

By _____

Playground Code

Do you like playing out? Is your playground a safe and friendly place? Write a paragraph saying what you like and what you do not like about your playground. Suggest any improvements you would like to introduce.

Write down six rules or suggestions that you would like to see introduced to ensure a happy and safe playground.

1.

2.

3.

4.

5.

6.

By ———————————————————

The Law of the Land

Just as rules are needed at home and at school, so it is necessary to have rules, in the form of laws, to enable the country to run smoothly and to be a safe place in which to live. Without such rules, life would be chaotic and our civilized society would break down. The Law of the land is laid down by Parliament and it is up to the people of the land to elect members of Parliament (M.P.s).

General Elections

The United Kingdom is divided up into areas known as *constituencies.* Each constituency is represented by one *Member of Parliament.* M.P.s are elected from the various candidates who put themselves forward. The candidates may be from a political party or an organisation that has paid the required deposit to stand. It is also possible to stand as an independent candidate.

Every United Kingdom citizen over the age of eighteen is eligible to vote. When a general election is held, polling stations are provided so that people can register their votes. These stations may be in schools, church halls or community halls. People who are unable to get to a polling station may apply to vote by post. Once they are in office, the Government can call a general election at any time within a five year period. The political party that polls the most votes is invited to form the Government. Other parties, together with any independent M.P.s form the Opposition.

How much do you know?

You may need to use the school library or the internet to find the answers to the following questions:-

Who is the present Prime Minister and which political party does he/she represent?

Can you name any previous Prime Ministers?

Who is the Chancellor of the Exchequer? What does the Chancellor of the Exchequer do?

Who is the leader of the main opposition party?

Who is your local M.P. and which political party does he/she represent?

Why are there different political parties?

The Criminal Justice System

The Criminal Justice System is the method by which the law is enforced. It is best explained by illustrating how a case progresses through the legal system:-

Investigation

Once a crime has been reported, it is the job of the police to investigate and try and solve the crime. It is also the role of the police to do everything they can to prevent crime.

Arrest

Once a suspect has been identified, the police may arrest that person or alternatively, the suspect may be summonsed before a court. When a suspect is arrested, that person is taken to a police station and put in a cell. The suspect may be interviewed in the presence of a solicitor. The police may then decide to charge the person with an offence, issue a formal caution or release the person with no further action.

Preparation for Court

Once a charge has been made, both the defence solicitor and the prosecutor will begin to prepare for court. Statements will be taken from any witnesses. The Crown Prosecutor will decide whether there is enough evidence to secure a conviction and, if this is the case, a prosecution will go ahead.

Magistrates' Court

The accused has to decide whether to plead guilty or not guilty before he/she appears before a magistrate in court. If a guilty plea is put forward, the magistrate will pass sentence immediately. A plea of not guilty means that the magistrate has to listen to the evidence before making a decision. About 95% of all cases are decided in the Magistrates' Court.

Crown Court

A Crown Court trial is held before a judge and a jury. Once the jury has been sworn in, the prosecutor opens and gives all the evidence against the defendant. The defence then puts forward its evidence. Both sides are allowed to cross-examine each other's witnesses. Finally, the judge sums up the case and the jury retires to consider its verdict. Once the jury has decided, the jurors return to court and the verdict is announced. If the defendant is found not guilty, he/she is discharged immediately. However, if the defendant is found guilty, the judge passes sentence.

The Sentence

It is up to the judge to pass sentence, having taken account of the facts and circumstances of the offender. The judge can order any one of four levels of sentence. These are: a discharge, a fine, a period of community service, a period of imprisonment. It is most common for a judge to issue a fine. Imprisonment is the most severe sentence and is only enforced for serious offences.

The Youth Court

If a crime is committed by someone under the age of eighteen, they may be summoned to appear before the Youth Court. Youth offenders are subject to different rules than adults and are seldom sent before a Crown Court. Parents of young offenders can be issued with court orders to prevent their children re-offending.

Activities/Points for Discussion

It is the role of the police to do everything possible to prevent crime. Who else can help in this role? In what ways can crime be prevented?

Why do you think it is important to be honest from an early age?

Do you think the 'jury system' in Crown Court is a good idea? Why?

Should serious offenders be sent to prison? What are the advantages and disadvantages of sending people to prison?

What is 'Community Service'? Is this a good idea?

A Crown Court is presided over by a judge...
been written in the presence of jurors and given... the...
material. The defence then puts forward its case, then calling its own key
to cross examine, again offered witnesses... finally, the judge sums up the case
giving the jury the arguments to consider. Once it is a jury is satisfied, then an
option to bring about the verdict is announced. If the defendant is found not
guilty, he is discharged immediately. However, if the defendant is found
guilty the judge passes sentence.

The Sentence

In deciding upon a sentence, having taken
account of the facts and circumstances of the
offender, the judge consider any circumstances of the
sentence. These can include a fine, a period of
community service, a period of imprisonment. Imprisonment is the
common for a judge to issue on the imprisonment is a
the most severe sentence and is only reserved for
serious offences.

the Youth Court

A Youth is committed by someone between the age of eighteen. They may be
summoned to appear before the Youth Court. Youth offences are dealt with
differently from adults and the decision makers are different. Youth Court
primarily operate on the basis of ways youth offenders to prevent the children re
offending.

Activities/Points for Discussion

Is the role of the police to do everything because to protect them or no. Who
else can help in this role? In what ways can crime be prevented?

Why do you think it is important to be honest from an early age?

Do you think the law is fair in Crown plea is upheld plea. Why?

Should anyone go to prison prison. What are the disadvantages
and advantages of sending people to prison?

When is community service is it necessary?

Bullying

No matter how good, caring and well organised a school is, there are inevitably occasions when bullying takes place. It is important that such incidents are not ignored, either by the victims, other children, members of staff or parents. Bullying needs to be tackled quickly and effectively so that it can be stopped permanently. It is the responsibility of every child and adult in school to create and maintain a bully free environment.

What is bullying?

There are many different types of bullying. It can take the form of one or two isolated incidents or it can go on for a long period of time. It can include physical abuse – e.g. hitting, kicking, pushing etc., verbal abuse – e.g. insults, name calling etc., or isolation – e.g. ignoring the victim and encouraging others to do the same. Sometimes it is difficult for people to recognise bullying, as it can be very subtle.

Whatever form bullying takes it may be defined as:
Deliberate action to hurt, threaten or frighten an intended victim.

Bullying can be perpetrated by an individual, a couple of people or a 'bully gang', with one or two obvious leaders and a group of followers. Bullies enjoy the feeling of power and control over their victims. They may be unpopular themselves even though they appear to have a lot of friends.

Discussion and Follow Up

Identify as many different types/examples of bullying as possible. Make a list on a board or flipchart.

Talk about different examples of bullying. Is there one form of bullying worse than any other?

Has anyone been in a position where they have felt threatened and frightened? What happened?

'Bullying can take the form of isolation.' What does this mean?

How can bullying be *'very subtle'*? Can you think of any examples?

What do you think makes somebody a bully? Why would someone deliberately want to hurt or upset another person?

Why might an unpopular bully seem to have many friends?

What Should You Do If You Are A Victim?

Bullying can make your life a misery. Bullying could also affect your health and your progress at school. If you are bullied you might be so worried and frightened that you have problems sleeping; you might experience stomach aches, headaches or sickness; you might not want to eat or you might want to eat all the time for comfort. All of these effects contribute to make the situation worse.

The worst thing you can do is ignore the bullying and hope that it goes away. If you are being bullied you need to take some action.

YOU SHOULD:

• Walk quickly and confidently away from any incident, if this is possible.

• Try to avoid situations where you are alone with a known bully. Bullies always pick on people who are in a weaker position than themselves.

• Tell an adult. This should be someone who is in a position to take action on your behalf. It could be a teacher, a classroom assistant or a lunchtime supervisor.

• Be honest with the adult and say exactly how you feel. If you are really frightened – say so!

• Talk to a friend about your situation. It always helps to share a problem and your friend might be able to give you good advice.

• Tell your parents. Explain the situation to whoever looks after you at home. Your parents may wish to contact school to discuss the problem.

Never be tempted to be a bully. Put yourself in the place of the victim and imagine just how awful you would feel.

Discussion and Follow Up

Where and when do bullies pick on their victims? Does bullying always take place in a quiet corner of the playground or is it sometimes more open?

Is it possible for bullying to take place in the classroom? Give examples.

How might bullying affect a victim's progress at school?

Why might a victim hesitate to tell an adult about bullying?

Do you think adults ever get bullied? How might this happen?

Would You Walk By On The Other Side?

SCENARIO:

On several occasions, you have noticed Dean and Susie, two Year 6 pupils, picking on Michael, a younger pupil, in the school playground. Dean and Susie have also threatened other children and warned them not to play with Michael. So far you have ignored the situation, even though Michael has clearly looked frightened and you have seen him standing on his own, crying. One lunchtime, you spot Dean and Susie dragging Michael around the side of the school building so that they are all out of sight. Michael is doing his best to escape but they are too strong. You hesitate for a moment and then decide to take some action. **BUT WHAT SHOULD YOU DO?**

Think about:

What could happen if you ignore the situation.

What you would do first.

Who you would approach in the first instance.

What you would tell the person you approach.

How else you might help Michael.

Now:

Write your own short story about bullying. The bullying can take any form you wish and the action does not have to be confined to school. Your story should be a 'moral tale' from which others could learn about the consequences of bullying.

Work in groups to produce a short piece of drama on the theme of bullying. Each group should present the drama to the rest of the class.

Peer Pressure

What is 'peer pressure'?

When you are with a group of friends, it is very easy to be tempted to do something you do not really want to do – something you know to be wrong. If everyone else in the group seems to be in agreement, it is easier to go along with the suggestion even though your conscience might tell you otherwise. After all, you don't want to appear a spoilsport, do you? This is known as *peer pressure* and the wrong type of peer pressure could lead you into danger or serious trouble.

Everyone needs friends and it is fun to be part of a larger group – but sometimes you have to be strong and say 'no' if others try to persuade you to do something you know to be wrong. Follow you conscience and have the courage to resist peer pressure. If *your* friends constantly encourage you to do things that you know to be wrong then you have chosen the wrong group of friends.

Discussion

Have you ever been in a situation where you have experienced peer pressure? What did you do? Talk about your situation.

What should you do?

Read and discuss the different scenarios outlined below. What might the consequences be in each example if you give in to peer pressure? What do you think you would do in each situation?

• You are on your way to school with a group of friends. A couple of your friends decide to visit the local newsagents to buy some crisps and sweets. Once inside, you see one of your friends take a pen from a display. Another of your classmates puts some chewing gum into his pocket without paying for it. When you leave the shop, they tell you how easy it was and they encourage you to go back inside and try for yourself.

- It is a warm summer evening and you are playing out with your friends. Your best friend's older brother turns up and offers you some cigarettes. He explains that smoking is cool and makes you look grown up. Your best friend accepts one and encourages you to do the same.

- You are on holiday from school and a group of you decide to play ball in the school playground. Before long, the ball is thrown onto the school roof. Your friends tell you it is easy to climb onto the school roof and one of them shows you how it is done. Your friend signals for the rest of the group to follow.

- You are walking home from a sports event with some of your team mates. One of them suggests taking a shortcut across a railway track, as there is a hole in the security fencing. The others agree and begin to make their way towards the gap. In the distance, a train can be heard approaching.

Now:

See if you can make up a scenario of your own. Discuss the situation and talk about the consequences.

Work in a group to act out your scenario. When you have practised, perform your drama to the rest of the class.

Can you write a story about a character who experiences peer pressure? You will need to:

- Place your character in a difficult situation.

- Think about the other characters in your story.

- Work out the consequences of the action.

- Decide how to end your story.

Smoking

As you grow older you will have to make many difficult choices and decisions. It is almost certain that you will mix with people who choose to smoke. You may already have an older brother or sister, or some friends who smoke. The same people might encourage you to try cigarettes, giving you all sorts of reasons why you should smoke. What will you do? Before you make a decision it is as well to know the facts about smoking.

The Facts

- In the United Kingdom, smoking kills 13 people every hour. This means that smoking kills over 120,000 in the U.K. every year.

- Currently, there are about 13 million adult smokers in the United Kingdom. The number of adult smokers has dropped since the 1950's and 1960's but information gained over the last few years points to another upward trend.

- The number of children and young people who smoke is increasing steadily.

- The upward trend amongst young smokers is especially notable among girls. Figures show that 1 in 3 15-year old girls smoke regularly.

- Smoking is addictive and those who begin smoking young often go on to smoke for the rest of their lives. Figures show that 82 per cent of smokers take up the habit as teenagers.

The Risks

- Clearly, most people know that smoking is bad for their health. Smoking cuts people's life expectancy. People who smoke regularly and die of a smoking-related disease lose on average 16 years from their life expectancy compared to non-smokers.

- Smoking is the prime cause of cancer and heart disease. It also causes many other fatal conditions and chronic illnesses among adults.

- Half of all the people who continue to smoke for most of their lives die through smoking related illnesses.

- The younger people start to smoke, the greater the risk. People who start smoking when they are young are more likely to smoke for longer and to **die** early from smoking. Someone who starts smoking at 15 is 3 times more likely to die from cancer than someone who starts smoking in their mid 20's.

Passive Smoking

Passive smoking occurs through breathing in other people's tobacco smoke. Have you ever been in a room where other people are smoking? You cannot help but breathe in the smoke from their cigarettes. The same smoke often makes your eyes sting. It is not a very pleasant experience.

Passive smoking can also be a killer. Most non-smokers are not at risk as they are not continually exposed to passive smoking. However, a significant number of people may be at risk. For example, those who live with smokers or those who work in particularly smoky atmospheres may well suffer as a result of passive smoking.

Passive smoking almost certainly contributes to deaths from both lung cancer and heart disease and even low levels of passive smoking can cause illness. For example, those who suffer from asthma are more prone to attacks when exposed to a smoky atmosphere. Children who are asthma sufferers are particularly vulnerable. Figures issued by The Royal College of Physicians show that '*17,000 hospital admissions in a single year of children under 5 are due to their parents smoking*'. Furthermore, women who smoke during pregnancy are likely to reduce the birth weight and damage the health of their baby.

Discussion

It is clear that most children and young people know that smoking is dangerous and can permanently damage their health. Why, then, do young people begin to smoke? Discuss this in a group and see how many reasons you can find.

Why do you think adults, who should know better, continue to smoke?

Have you ever stood or sat next to someone who is a heavy smoker? Your senses will soon warn you if you are near such a person! What do you notice?

Activities

Design and produce a classroom display warning about the risks of smoking. Your display should provide both facts and opinions. Include pictures so that your display is visually effective. For example, a large picture of a smoker on one side of your display could contrast with a healthy non-smoker on the other side.

Design anti-smoking posters. Bold posters with a clear and straightforward message are always more effective. Display your posters in key areas around school. Be sure to include an area that is visited by parents and other adults.

Work in small groups to produce a piece of drama related to smoking. For example, your work could show how a young person reacts when tempted by others to smoke. When you have practised, perform your piece for the rest of the class. Can any of the work be adapted for school assembly?

REMEMBER – do not start smoking.

BE STRONG ENOUGH TO SAY 'NO!'

Caring for the Environment

What is vandalism?

Vandalism is the deliberate act of defacing, damaging
or destroying property or belongings. The implications
of vandalism can be very serious. At its worst,
vandalism can threaten life and, indeed, many people
are killed or seriously injured every year due to the
irresponsible behaviour of vandals. In addition, the annual
cost to the country, in terms of repair and replacement of
property, is regularly over a hundred million pounds.

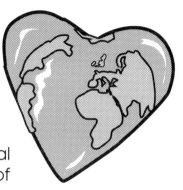

*It is important that you learn to look after your own property and respect the
property of others from an early age.*

What do *you* do if you see some coats on the floor in the cloakroom? Do you
hang them up or do you walk over them?

What do *you* do if you notice that some P.E. equipment has been left outside
in the rain? Do you bring it in or do you run for shelter?

What do *you* do if you realise that some books have fallen from a shelf onto the
classroom floor? Do you put them back or ignore them until the teacher
notices?

Discussion and Follow Up

What are the possible implications for the following acts of vandalism?

Vandals push a rubbish bin up to the school entrance and set fire to the
contents.

A public telephone kiosk is smashed and the phone is destroyed.

Teenagers climb onto a school roof, rip the felt covering and jump onto a
glass skylight.

Vandals break through the protective fencing leading to a railway track.
They throw objects, including bricks and tree branches, onto the railway
line.

All the windows at a school Nursery are smashed and the glass is scattered
over the books and play equipment inside.

How much do you care?

SCENARIO:

There are just eight days to go to the school Christmas holiday. Your class has been working hard on Christmas activities for the past two weeks. All the children have made lovely cards and calendars for their parents, the room has been decorated and the Christmas display work looks superb. You are really proud of the work you and your classmates have produced.

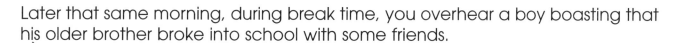

You come in to school one cold and frosty morning to discover that vandals have broken in through a window and wrecked the classroom. The walls have been sprayed with paint, the decorations have been torn down and the Christmas cards and calendars have been ripped up and scattered. In addition, your schoolbooks have been thrown on the floor and trampled on.

Later that same morning, during break time, you overhear a boy boasting that his older brother broke into school with some friends.

EITHER:

Write a paragraph to say how you feel when you first enter the classroom. How do you feel towards the vandals? Would you take any action after your playtime discovery? What would you do?

OR:

Turn the scenario into a full story. You could write the story in the first person or you could invent your own characters. What happens at the end of your story? Do you work even harder to tidy and restore the classroom? Do the vandals get caught?

Graffiti

Graffiti is a form of vandalism. Your first thoughts may be that graffiti is not too serious. However, graffiti can make a building or a whole area look run down and uncared for. Furthermore, a building covered with graffiti is often a target for other forms of vandalism.

Vandals who daub or spray graffiti onto walls and buildings are usually not very bright. For example, sometimes they sign their names so that it is obvious who has committed the vandalism! They often put themselves in great danger by trying to leave graffiti high up on buildings or even on motorway bridges. Hospitals have had to treat vandals who have fallen from a great height in their efforts to leave their mark.

Cleaning up graffiti costs a great deal of money that could be better used to improve facilities in the environment.

Is there any graffiti around your school? What could you do to make people realise that this is unacceptable?

Litter

Dropping litter is another form of vandalism – although many people do not see it as such. You may not think that you are doing any harm dropping the occasional piece of paper or chocolate bar wrapper – but if everyone dropped litter instead of using waste bins our country would be filthy. Furthermore, litter can be dangerous to both people and wildlife. Have you ever arrived at school in the morning to find that a bottle has been smashed in your playground? Imagine how dangerous a broken bottle could be if it was left on a beach or in a farmer's field. Plastic bags and tin cans are just as dangerous to birds and animals. In some areas, hypodermic needles are left lying around. If ever you find a hypodermic needle, do not touch it. Inform an adult immediately so that it can be dealt with correctly.

Litter can lead to more serious pollution. Imagine if you just threw all of your litter on the floor at home. Your house would soon be covered with rubbish and rotten food. It would attract mice and rats and it would smell awful! Yet people continue to dump their rubbish, often on the nearest piece of land they can find. Old tyres, discarded furniture and even wrecked cars are left for others to deal with. Rivers and streams can become polluted and the local wildlife is affected.

Remember:
Caring for the environment is everybody's responsibility.

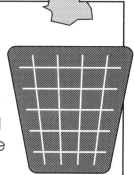

Discussion and Follow Up

Take a look around your classroom. Is it tidy? Is there litter on the floor or on the shelves and bookcases? Has your classroom rubbish gone in the bin or is it on the floor around the bin? You could appoint monitors on a rota system to make sure your classroom is a **Litter Free Zone.**

Identify **key areas** around your school that are more likely to attract litter. For example, paper towels might litter the floor near washbasins or drinking fountains; entrances or cloakroom areas might be untidy. **What can you do to improve these areas? How can you educate others not to drop litter?**

Carry out a litter survey around the school grounds. Do different areas attract different types of litter? Which areas are most vulnerable? Your survey can be followed by a 'clean up campaign'. Be sure to wear plastic gloves if you are collecting litter – and you still need to wash your hands thoroughly when you have finished.

Design anti-litter posters to encourage others not to drop litter. Your posters can be displayed in prominent positions around school.

Talk to your older brothers and sisters, your parents and other adults about your **litter campaign.** Adults are often worse than children when disposing of litter!

Feelings and Emotions

Everybody experiences a whole range of different feelings and emotions – but what causes those feelings? Sometimes it is good to talk about your feelings and share your emotions with others. Talking about your emotions can help you understand them and so you can deal with them in a better way.

How many feelings and emotions can you identify? Collect together as many as you can on a whiteboard or flipchart. Here are a few to start you off:

 **anger**

boredom

Feelings and Emotions

 **love**

fear

- What causes your feelings and emotions? What is it that makes you happy, or sad, or angry? Discuss this in a group.

- Choose six feelings and emotions and write a sentence to illustrate each one.
  e.g. I feel angry when my little brother always gets his own way.

- Now choose just one emotion and write more fully about an experience. For example, you might write about an event that made you really happy, or an experience that frightened you.

- Can you experience more than one emotion at once? For example, can you feel anger towards someone and yet still love them? Have you ever felt scared and yet excited? Think of as many examples as you can and talk about them in a group. Perhaps you could write about your experiences.

Strong Emotions

Identify six strong emotions from the collection of feelings and emotions you have already made. One person, or the teacher, should write the choices on six separate cards. **(Good examples of strong emotions are anger, jealousy, hate etc.)** Talk about these emotions in a class group or in circle time. What made you angry, jealous etc.? Try to describe exactly **how** you felt inside. How did you feel towards other people involved?

The class should be divided into six smaller groups – five or six children to a group is perfect. One person from each group should come out and select an **emotion card.** Each group has to make up a short drama sequence to illustrate the emotion. This should take fifteen to twenty minutes, following which, the scenes should be performed for all to see.

After each short performance, discuss the content with the rest of the class. The audience may wish to question the actors or make comments.

> **Could your class present an assembly about emotions?**
> **Are any of the scenes good enough to perform for the**
> **rest of the school?**

Dealing With Your Emotions

Some strong emotions may tempt you to act in a certain way. For example, if someone makes you angry, you might be tempted to hit out at him/her. This is clearly wrong and there could be serious consequences – you could hurt someone badly and you could get into trouble as a result. However, if something happens to make you really sad – perhaps someone very close to you dies – you may find that crying helps you to cope.

Can you think of any other examples?

As you grow up, you have to learn to deal with your emotions. Sometimes it is very difficult. Discuss ways of controlling or dealing with your emotions? What should you do if you are very angry, or jealous, or feel hate towards someone? Does it help to have someone you can talk to? Is it important to have close, reliable friends?

Emotional Poems

Can you write an *Emotional Poem?* Choose *one* feeling or emotion and begin by making *a list of causes.* For example, if you choose *happiness,* think of lots of different things that make you happy.

As an example, here is the start of a poem about jealousy:

Jealousy Is .....

Jealousy is watching my dad playing with my little sister and leaving me out.
Jealousy is listening to my friend Danny telling me about his fantastic summer holiday in Florida.
Jealousy is driving to school in our next-door neighbour's brand new car.
Jealousy is watching Charlie Higgins sit next to the lovely Laura Larkin every day in class.
Jealousy is ......

When you have finished your poem make a good, neat, illustrated copy. Your emotional poems should make an effective classroom display.

Other People's Feelings

Are you sensitive to others? Do you appreciate that other people experience the same feelings and emotions as you? Have you ever said something to someone that 'hurts his/her feelings'? Have you ever deliberately left someone out of a game or playground discussion?

It is important to learn to respect other people's feelings. A good rule as to how to live your life is to treat others as you yourself would like to be treated.

Activity: Can you write a short story about a character who is hurt by others?

What happens to hurt your character? How does your character feel?

What does your character do? Who does your character turn to? Do those who hurt your character learn from the experience?

Good Relationships

Do you get on well with people? Do you find that others are eager to be in your company – or do you find that friends and family try to avoid you because they find you difficult? Throughout your life you will meet people and form new relationships - relationships with your immediate family, other relatives, school friends, people you meet outside school, work colleagues, a marriage partner. Your ability to relate to people will have a major effect on how successful you are in life and, more importantly, will be a major factor in determining how happy you are in your life.

Your Family

Do you like being at home? Do you like spending time with your family? A happy home relies on co-operation from family members. It is important that everyone helps at home and supports each other. Sometimes, specific jobs might be allocated to different members of the family. For example, there might be a 'washing up rota'. There may be times when you feel that such jobs are a chore but, when family members do not co-operate and play their part in the running of the home, problems may occur. Nobody likes to live in an environment where there are constant arguments and co-operation from all family members is the key to a happy home.

Activities and Points for Discussion

What jobs are you expected to do regularly at home?

Do you ever volunteer to do extra jobs? If so, what are they?

What makes your parents get annoyed with you?

Are there any things that annoy you at home?

Identify five positive things about your life at home?

Write about a really good day that you have enjoyed with your family. It could be when you were on holiday, a birthday or even Christmas Day. However, it could just be an ordinary day that turned out to be special in some way.

Your Friends

Do you make friends easily? Do you *like* the friends you already have or would you prefer to have different friends? How do you think your friends feel about you? Take a close look at yourself – would you like to be your friend?

Everyone likes to be popular. It is lovely to have lots of friends – but it is equally important to choose the right sort of friends. You do not want to get into trouble by choosing friends who might lead you astray. You should think about the qualities you want in a friend – and then think if you have those qualities yourself!

Activities and Points for Discussion

What qualities do you want in a friend? Make a list of all the things you look for when choosing a friend.

Are some qualities more important than others? Look again at your list and rearrange the points in order of priority.

Why do you think it is so important to have friends? What sort of things do you do with your friends?

Do you have a special friend? Write all about one of your friends who is special to you. Mention all the good qualities your friend has – and perhaps one or two things that you find annoying about your friend! (Be sure not to write anything hurtful!)

Have you ever had an argument with your best friend? How did you feel? How was the problem resolved?

Write a poem entitled MY BEST FRIEND. You can write about your friend's qualities and about the things you do together. You could draw a picture of your friend and write your finished poem beneath.

Good Manners

Have you noticed the number of people who display bad manners? The sad thing is that many of them are adults who should know better! Well-mannered people produce a well-mannered society in which citizens are polite and helpful. It is important to learn good habits when you are young and not to follow the bad example of others.

There are times when children display bad manners because they break the rules:

> **e.g.** **Talking when the teacher is addressing the class.**
> **Walking around in class instead of remaining seated.**
> **Disrupting other children in school assembly.**

Can you think of further examples of bad manners? Perhaps you have seen examples of bad manners in and around school. Make a list on a whiteboard or flip chart.

Discuss the examples on your list. Are there any examples where displaying bad manners could be dangerous?

> **e.g.** **Barging through a crowded doorway.**

Activity 1

Bad Mannered Bob and Well Mannered Mike are in the same class at school. However, they are almost complete opposites. Write a character study for each of them. You might wish to describe briefly how each character looks – but you should concentrate on the way they behave. You can write about the things they do both at home and at school. Produce your work in rough first of all and then draw a picture of each character and write your finished description underneath.

Now:
Can you write a story or a short play in which Bad Mannered Bob and Well Mannered Mike are the main characters? You will need to plan your work before you begin. Perhaps it could be a moral tale in which Bob learns the errors of his ways.

Activity 2

You would probably not want to make friends with the girl in the following scene. Read the extract carefully and identify all the examples of bad manners.

As the children of Brick Street School lined up patiently by the hall door, Mandy Midgely rushed out of her classroom and pushed her way in at the front of the queue.

'Hey! That's not fair!' protested Rebecca, one of her classmates. 'We've been waiting for ages!'

'Tough!' snapped Mandy. 'I'm starving. Why should I wait at the back of the queue? Anyway, it's stupid queuing up. What's the point?'

Mrs Henderson, the lunchtime supervisor opened the hall door and Mandy barged through, stepping on Mrs Henderson's foot in her haste to get to the serving hatch.

'It wasn't my fault,' said Mandy, as Mrs Henderson hopped up and down on one leg. 'You should have got your foot out of the way!'

Mandy dodged past three more children so that she was at the very front of the queue.

'What's for dinner?' she asked, peering over the counter. She sniffed and wiped her nose on the back of a very dirty hand. ' I hope it's better than yesterday.'

'Would you like sausage and mash or cheese salad?' said Mrs Banks, with a smile.

'I'll have sausage and mash,' said Mandy. 'Give me lots, will you – I'm starving.'

Mrs Banks served Mandy and passed the plate over the counter. Mandy took it without a word and sat down at the nearest table, glaring at one of the infant children who sat opposite her. Mandy coughed loudly, picked up her fork and began to shovel her dinner into her mouth. The infant opposite took one look at her eating and put his knife and fork back on his plate. He'd had enough dinner for that day.

Now:
See if you can improve Mandy's manners! Rewrite the passage so that Mandy becomes a well-mannered and considerate child. Quite a challenge!